CROSS TRAINING

A SPORTS DEVOTIONAL

WIN DAVIS & CALVIN DUNCAN

Copyright © 2010 by Win Davis and Calvin Duncan
Cover illustrated by Susie Fife.

Scripture taken from the HOLY BIBLE, NEW INTERNATIONAL VERSION®, NIV®. Copyright © 1973, 1978, 1984 by International Bible Society. Used by permission of Zondervan. All rights reserved.

ISBN 978-0-7414-6268-8

Printed in the United States of America

Published November 2012

INFINITY PUBLISHING

Toll-free (877) BUY BOOK
Local Phone (610) 941-9999
Fax (610) 941-9959
Info@buybooksontheweb.com
www.buybooksontheweb.com

We always give thanks to God for all of you and mention you in our prayers constantly! *(1 Thessalonians 1:2)*

The wise writer of Proverbs noted "As iron sharpens iron, so one person sharpens another (Proverbs 27:17)." There could not be a more appropriate scripture verse as we reflect on every one of our teammates. Not just the ones on the courts and playing field of our athletic pasts (although you certainly raised the level of our play), we're referring to the many people who have contributed to making our lives as athletes, coaches, writers, ministers, and just imperfect believers, better for the many times you provided good coaching, support, encouragement, and correction. To note everyone's contribution would possibly double the size of this book of devotions, thus we shall be brief knowing we have "dropped the ball" when it comes to thanking everyone and highlighting their many contributions. We just want you to know that at this time, it's our turn to be your fans as we cheer on your hopes, dreams, ministries, and life.

From Calvin

To my wonderful wife, Barbara, and children Richard, Chelsea and Azell. It's truly a blessing to have all of you by my side. To my (dearly departed) mother and my Aunt Mable – You were my angels sent from the Lord. To Mrs. Isner – Where would I be if you and Mr. Isner hadn't taken me into your home...and into your heart? To my church family at Faith and Family Church – In half a dozen years of ministry, God has exceeded all of my expectations. You guys are the best! - And to Bishop Daniel Robertson, and Mt. Gilead for providing the 'church key.' To my Spiritual mentors Steve Parson, Steve Stells, Bishop Wellington Boone, and Dr. Bryan E. Crute – Any impact I have on others can be traced to your influence on me. My co-author Win Davis – Thanks for the assist and for being my constant encourager. To the coaching staff at VCU, JD Barnette, Orlando "Tubby" Smith, Kevin Eastman, and Dave Hobbs for everything that you have taught me. Coach Anthony Grant for allowing me the opportunity to come back and be a part of the basketball 'team' as their life coach. Coach Harley 'Skeeter' Swift who helped hone my skills at Oak Hill Academy. What can I say, but, "No one sweeter than Skeeter." Coach Lorenzo Romar – From AIA to the Pros, you are my John the Baptist. Norwood Teague, who was instrumental in incorporating me into the VCU athletics program. To Rolando Lamb aka "America's Character Coach" – Our friendship on and off the court is second to none. To my 'little brother' Don Franco, who inspired me to start writing. To Susie Fife – For your God-given talent in designing our book cover and so much more. Lisa Schyler – God sent you my way and I am blessed for all you have done. And finally to Jeff and Tracy Street, who believed in me and helped me to see the bigger picture.

From Win

Debbie, Love/Love began both our tennis game and our marriage. My prayer is that we continue serving and receiving. Andi and Malika – Dad is the greatest coaching job I could ever have. I love you and will always be your biggest fan in all you do. To my parents Reid and Kathleen – For always being my biggest fans. Joe Williams and April Stinson – For inviting me to youth camp, where I accepted Jesus Christ as Lord & Savior. Arthur Drago – The discipline of 5:30 AM meditation, and many encouraging postcards. Dean John Kinney and the STVU faculty at Virginia Union University – For affirming a historical and colorblind Jesus. Coach Guy Walton – For taking a chance on "Old School." Coach Steve Baker – Spaghetti, Kool-Aid and FCA. Coach Bob Myers – For making me believe I could play at the next level. Coach 'B' (aka Ira Blumenthal) – My writing & speaking "Solomon in the Wise." Bonnie Surma – The talent and 'patience' to get this book done. Randy & Carolyn Graham – For a 'variety' of freshly squeezed juices during my '40 days in the wilderness.' Pastor Allan Mitchell – Praying, fasting and mentoring. George Kupets – Bagels, Nutella and motivation to pursue my passion. Pastor Chris Robbins – For keeping me accountable. Cambridge Baptist Youth and Young Adults – For keeping 'The World's Oldest Youth Pastor' young. You are awesome! Bill Broscious and Craig Mattice – Living fully in the face of death. The Lamda Chi Alpha - Phi Eta chapter at James Madison University – Teaching me servant-leadership. Pastor, Life Coach, co-author and friend Calvin Duncan – We did it 'buddy!' And to my niece and marathoner Sarah Lynn Bergquist – For your courage as you crossed the finish line to Heaven first.

And most importantly to our Lord & Savior Jesus Christ

You have surely bestowed upon us more blessings than we deserve and given us the incredible responsibility to "Preach the Gospel" in our words and actions on and off the court and field of play. Please forgive us for the many times we have dropped the ball, as our brother Paul wrote, to "press on toward the goal for the prize of the upward call of God in Christ Jesus."

Sports have been an important part of history for thousands of years. In times of distress and world crises, sports have given people hope and a distraction from challenging times. Even during times of war, countries have laid down their weapons to participate in athletic competition.

One of the greatest writers of all time, whose words have been translated into virtually every known language in the world and whose chapters have been read by literally billions of people, often used sports to describe life changing events. He alluded to the intensity of competition, the desire to win a championship, the necessity of pushing one's self to perform and the down side of over-training. He often carried his message to a sports-obsessed society and, in the end, let them know that as important as sports are, there is something much, much greater. As both athletes and Christians, we believe this writer, more commonly referred to as The Apostle Paul, was guided by Jesus Christ and the Holy Spirit of God. By no means would we dare to compare the analogies in this book to some of the greatest writings of all time. We are, however, a couple thousand years later, still living in a sports-obsessed society. Our hope and prayer is that the analogies we have observed between sports and faith will encourage you to open God's word (the Bible), to discover and apply the greatest 'coaching' you will ever receive. Or, as our brother Paul might suggest, to "run straight to the goal with purpose in every step" (1 Corinthians 9:26).

Body, Mind & Spirit – A Game Plan for this Sports Devotion

Whether you are an experienced veteran, rookie, or beginner in your faith-walk, this sports devotion book is designed to help you understand how the Bible applies to your life. But even more importantly, how you can join God's team of Christians (we were going to say The Saints, but that would have been a little too obvious). Each of these devotions contain seven short sections.

Headline & Sports Report – The beginning of every devotion tells a brief story about something we've observed in sports or experienced as athletes. We think you'll not only find these interesting, but, hopefully, applicable to your own life as an athlete, fan, and/or observer of the connection between life and sports.

Sports Analogy – The paragraph that follows the sport's story compares the short story you just read to an event and/or lesson from the Bible (which is taken from the passage highlighted in the *TIME OUT* section).

TIME OUT – On the scoreboard at the bottom of the pages, we've highlighted quotes from the Bible. We've used different translations that we believe accurately express the intention and spirit of the passage. And, therefore, a Bible verse that is relevant to your life today.

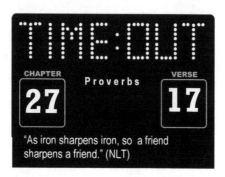

Body – The Body section under the CROSS TRAINING banner offers coaching for improving your physical fitness and/or successfully performing as an athlete. It is important to remember that these are just guidelines based on our experiences as athletes and advice we've received over the years. God made everyone of us different; we all have different strengths and weaknesses. ***Do not attempt these exercises if you have limitations, injuries, restrictions, etc., that may hurt your health and wellness.***

Spirit – Also under the CROSS TRAINING banner is the Spirit section. This is one of the most important parts of your walk with God. This brief section offers advice regarding effective ways to draw closer to the Lord.

Mind – We believe the Mind section is also essential in your walk with God. It encourages you to read beyond the short scripture verse in the TIME OUT section, and urges you to spend time in the Bible learning from the greatest 'life' coaches ever gathered together to write the greatest playbook ever.

Journal – Would you stop playing a game with only a few minutes left until the end? Of course not! That is why we encourage you to finish each devotion by spending some time writing down your thoughts on the blank lines in the Journal section. It has been proved over and over again that actually writing down your thoughts, plans, and actions improve your chances of acting on the thought. Neglecting to record your thoughts is similar to missing an important part of your workout or to not putting proven plays in your game plan. Yes, just reading the devotion is helpful, but writing and internalizing what you've read offers much greater benefits and rewards. (Lines are provided for your journal entries.)

_____

_____

_____

_____

_____

Devoted to the Game

There's a popular expression in sports – "Devoted to the game." It suggests a commitment and passion for a particular sport i.e. "Devoted to the game of baseball, basketball, tennis, etc. As you read this book and come to know us, you will certainly come to realize that we are "devoted to the game." We love just about everything that is good in sports. We love the competition, the preparation, the excitement, etc. We love to play and we love to cheer on our favorite teams and players. We love to push and challenge our bodies, minds and spirits to perform at the highest level possible. We are devoted to the game and hope you enjoy our reflections and observations about sports, but dramatically more important is our desire and prayer that you see that's sports is only the means God has given us to share the greatest news in the history of the world – the Gospel (or Good News) of Jesus Christ. Our hope is that by the end of this sport's devotional as you read and internalize the final *'Game Plan of Salvation,'* you will be blessed with new information and inspiration to perform at the highest level on the greatest team ever assembled – God's Team!

Cross Training 4 Life

Iron Sharpens Iron

Beginning my freshman year as a basketball player at Virginia Commonwealth University, the coaching staff insisted on a grueling year-round training schedule - even during summer break. During this training, the coaching staff paired each of us with a teammate. I was paired with Rolando Lamb, who had been one the best high school players in Virginia. I soon realized that if I wanted to be successful on the collegiate level, I needed someone like Rolando to sharpen my skills and hold me accountable. The coaches knew Rolando and I were right for each other. As iron sharpens iron, Rolando and I sharpened each other. By our senior year, VCU was ranked one of the top college basketball programs in the country. Moreover, Rolando and I were honored by being selected All-Conference and All-American, respectively, and were recognized as one of the top guard tandems in the whole nation.

Together, we pushed each other on the court, but, far more important, is that years later Rolando and I still encourage each other as we motivate, mentor and minister in the name of Jesus Christ. As Christians, we all need to keep each other 'sharp' in our focus to be more like Jesus. We need to hold each other accountable for our words and actions, and help each other reach the full potential God has given us. We can do this by encouraging each other, praying for one another, and, even, rebuking each other when necessary. Remember, we are all on the same team. God is our coach, and the Bible is our playbook.

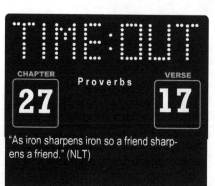

TIME:OUT

CHAPTER Proverbs VERSE

27 **17**

"As iron sharpens iron so a friend sharpens a friend." (NLT)

BODY

Train year-round to maximize your potential. Find (or have your coach suggest) another athlete who will push you and who wants to be pushed in return. Hold each other accountable and make "Iron sharpen Iron!"

SPIRIT

Pray this prayer: "Lord, Thank you for the blessings that you have given to me. Please send your Holy Spirit to guide my words and actions. Please allow me to be a blessing to others by giving me the words to encourage them and love them like You do. Amen."

MIND

Read verses 1 through 21 in Proverbs, chapter 27. Each of these involves relationships with other people. Write down three things you need to do to have a better relationship with Jesus Christ. Find a Christian friend who is willing to 'sharpen' you by keeping you accountable for your words and actions. Offer to be a 'true' Christian friend by keeping them accountable as well.

_____
_____
_____
_____
_____
_____
_____
_____
_____
_____
_____
_____
_____

Attitude Determines Altitude

During my freshman year of college, I became good friends with another first-year athlete named William. We had both been good high school athletes, and we each signed four-year scholarships to play college football for a team that had just competed for the small college national championship. As you can imagine, the level of competition was extremely high. Half a dozen players on our team would later play in the NFL. He couldn't wait for game day, and I dreaded it. The difference was in our attitudes.

William looked forward to every game we had while I was bitter and embarrassed that I was no longer the star. Although, neither of us got much playing time, he cheered while I sulked. He stuck it out. I quit and transferred to another university. A couple of years later I read in the newspaper that one of the guys who had sat on the bench with me had made All-Conference. You guessed it... William.

The Apostle Paul wrote that our attitude should be the same as Christ who humbled himself even though He was the very Son of God. As Paul notes, this humble servant-leader who sacrificed His life for you and me will one day be exalted for all to bow before.

How is your attitude? How are you treating others? Are you looking for ways to help someone other than yourself? Perhaps the first things you need to sacrifice so that you might serve God is your ego. Only then can you set an example by serving others.

TIME·OUT

CHAPTER **2** Philippians VERSE **5**

"Your attitude should be the same as that of Christ Jesus." (NIV)

BODY
Attitude beats aptitude when it comes to reaching altitude! Be coachable. Make a commitment to a positive and humble attitude as you train, play, practice, and support your teammates.

SPIRIT
Get one of those WWJD bracelets and wear it, *but* make sure the letters are facing you. Everyday be reminded in your attitude and actions– What Would Jesus Do?

MIND
Read and meditate on Philippians 2: 1-11. Journal some steps you could take so that your attitude could be more like Christ. Focus on others (including family) more than self.

_____

_____

_____

_____

_____

_____

_____

_____

_____

_____

_____

_____

_____

_____

Learn from Your Mistakes

The year before I was traded to the NBA's Chicago Bulls, the team had drafted another pretty good guard. You may have heard of this guy, Michael Jordan. Yeah - *that* Michael Jordan. One of the most popular ad campaigns run by Nike was a commercial titled "Failure." In it, Jordan reflects, "I've missed more than 9,000 shots in my career. I've lost almost 300 games. Twenty-six times, I've been trusted to take the game winning shot...and missed. I've failed over and over and over again in my life... and that's why I succeed." Part of Jordan's incredible success, was his ability to learn from the challenges he faced and to 'rebound' (pun intended) stronger and better as arguably the greatest basketball player ever to play the game.

What if a commercial was produced about our spiritual life instead of our athletic life? "I've sinned more than 9,000 times in my life. I've lost over 300 opportunities to share the Gospel of Jesus Christ. Too often, I've been trusted to serve those less fortunate...and missed the opportunity. I've failed over and over and over again in my life, and still, God has forgiven my sins. And that is why this time, I will succeed." The Bible tells us all have sinned and fallen short of God's perfection.

Part of being a good Christian is our willingness to learn from our mistakes. Accept the gift of God's forgiveness and emerge more determined to be stronger in your faith and service. Just do it!

TIME:OUT

CHAPTER
3

Romans

VERSE
23

"For all have sinned; all fall short of God's glorious standard." (NLT)

BODY
Commit to strengthening your weaknesses. Ask your coaches and teammates to point out areas you need to improve on, then work on them over and over again.

SPIRIT
Download the lyrics to Casting Crowns' "Voice of Truth." As you listen to the song, ask God to help you strengthen your spiritual weaknesses by praying specifically for the sins you are struggling with. Ask a close friend in Christ to pray for you and keep you accountable

MIND
Read Romans chapter 3:23-31. Journal your thoughts on what these verses mean to you. You may want to read a few different translations to better understand how they apply to your life.

_____

_____

_____

_____

_____

_____

_____

_____

_____

_____

_____

_____

_____

God's Bod

Unfulfilled potential. You may have heard this expression referring to an athlete with a great deal of promise who didn't fulfill expectations because of poor life choices. Those athletes had the sky as their limit, and yet somehow come crashing down to earth. Unfortunately, there are many examples, and most seem to revolve around drugs, alcohol, and/or inappropriate sexual relationships. When I was in college, one of my fellow athletes had been a high school All-American and made the varsity team's starting lineup his freshman year. But shortly thereafter, his girlfriend told him she was pregnant. Not wanting her to be a single mom, he left school and honorably married her. He had high hopes of returning to college, but it never worked out. Neither did the marriage, unfortunately. He had dreamed of becoming a coach, and I believe he would have been a great one. His poor choice cut short his potential, and now we will never know what great things he could have done.

The Bible is very clear about sex outside marriage. It is wrong. Jesus said that even looking upon one another with impure sexual thoughts puts us in danger of breaking God's commandment, "Do not commit adultery!" The Apostle Paul wrote that our bodies are temples belonging to God, and they are bought with a price. Keep this in mind, respect your body, resist sexual temptation, and demand respect from those who 'claim' to care about you. Fulfill your potential.

TIME:OUT

CHAPTER **6** 1 Corinthians VERSE **18**

"Run away from sexual sin! No other sin so clearly affects the body as this one does. For sexual immorality is a sin against your own body." (NLT)

CROSS TRAINING

BODY
Resistance bands are excellent additions to strength, training, and flexibility. These giant rubber bands or tubes keep constant tension on the muscle and allow a full range of motion. Check with a coach or a trainer on how resistance training can enhance your conditioning.

SPIRIT
Pray continually for the strength to honor God with your thoughts and actions: body, mind, and spirit.

MIND
Read 1 Corinthians 6:12-20. Journal the ways you should -and will- honor God with your body including proper diet, exercise, and sexual purity.

Trash Talking Belongs in The Trash

One of the best teams I played against in college was also one of the worst...in sportsmanship. During one match, the team's behavior was so boorish *their* coach chewed them out for their classlessness. Their antics screamed out, "Hey! Look at me! I'm so much better than you!"

Whether it's verbal jeers or an attitude of arrogance and superiority (note I didn't say confidence) when you compete, it's still the same thing - Trash Talking. You've probably heard it, maybe even been guilty of it. If you've taunted or disrespected your opponent, including celebrating overzealously (i.e. kicking your opponent when he or she is down), you're guilty of trash talking.

The Bible instructs us not to gloat when our enemy falls, and not to let our hearts rejoice. Even if you win, you've lost if your antics dishonor God and your Christian faith. Compete to win with all your God-given talent and desire. Next time, before you celebrate the victory, immediately go to your opponents and thank them for a good game. Help clean up sports by putting trash talking where it belongs...in the trash!

Oh, and by the way, that trash-talking team was humbled in a crushing defeat in the conference tournament by a team who spoke with action. What goes around comes around.

TIME:OUT

CHAPTER **PROVERBS** **VERSE**

24   17

"Do not gloat when your enemy falls; when he stumbles, do not let your heart rejoice." (NIV)

BODY
The best response to trash talking is outmatching it with the superior effort and determination acquired through hard work. Answer trash talking with silent in-your-face results on the court or field-of-play.

SPIRIT
Pray for the Holy Spirit to guide your words and actions as both a confident competitor and compassionate Christian.

MIND
Read Proverbs 24. Journal some wise actions you could take that would strengthen your body, your mind, and your relationship with Jesus Christ.

_____

_____

_____

_____

_____

_____

_____

_____

_____

_____

_____

_____

_____

Wisdom Builds A House

During my senior year of high school, I was recruited to play college football for a team who had just competed for the NAIA National Championship. The following year, my freshman year, we played for the conference championship despite losing a third of our starting lineup. Six of my teammates would later play in the NFL. More than the strengths of individual players, the key to our team's success was the wisdom of the coaching staff and their understanding of what it took to make small college athletics successful. Each coach had individual strengths: offense, defense, special teams, recruitment and, especially, development of their players' potential.

Like my coaches, the writer of Proverbs also knew that wisdom is needed to build a strong structure and that learning establishes a solid foundation. Each of us have individual strengths and talents that God expects us to use. As Christians, we need to seek the wisdom of God on how to use those strengths to build God's House (the team of believers called the church). We need to seek the Lord's understanding, and we need to strive to apply it to our lives and the lives of others. Jesus said in Matthew, chapter 7, verses 21-26, that everyone who puts His teaching into practice is like the wise man who builds his house on a solid foundation. With God as our coach, and His Word as our playbook, let's build a championship team together.

TIME OUT

CHAPTER **PROVERBS** VERSE

24 **3**

"By wisdom a house is built, and through understanding it is established." (NIV)

CROSS TRAINING

BODY
Protect your house! Practice beyond what is expected, and you will gain home court advantage. Know the course, the way the ball bounces, the tightness of the rim or net, every dip in the field, etc. Invite friends and family to your competitions (especially those at home) to give you and your teammates a little extra edge.

SPIRIT
Invite your teammates and coaches to join you for a prayer before your competition. Even if only one other person prays with you, Jesus said, "Where two or three or more are gathered in my name, I am there among them (Matthew 18:20)."

MIND
Read Proverbs 24. Write down 3 to 5 verses that could directly apply to your life. Journal about how the wisdom of these verses can help you make good choices, and, in so doing, help build your character.

_____

_____

_____

_____

_____

_____

_____

_____

_____

_____

_____

_____

_____

Eagles' Wings Trail Run

Almost every year I go to Wild, Wonderful West Virginia with my family for a little 'X-treme vacationing.' This generally includes activities such as hiking, mountain biking, trail running, horseback riding, whitewater rafting, and playing a few other outdoor sports. It can be exhausting. Yet, as I stumble, fall, flip, slip, and slide, there's something about the cool mountain air and refreshing water that keep me invigorated and looking forward to the next day's adventure.

The prophet Isaiah delivered a message to all Believers from God confirming the inevitability of human fatigue and imperfection. I believe Isaiah 40: 30 - 31 is saying, "Look, it's easy to get tired, burn out, or fall short of our potential. But when we're patient and keep our focus on God, we will be able to go that extra mile because the Lord is with us. He will give us the strength and endurance to accomplish the goals God has set for us. " How cool is that? Sure, we'll occasionally stumble, fall, slip, and slide, but God's there to pick us back up. This is especially important when we live and share our faith in Jesus Christ. We need Him to help us take on the challenges we face on a regular basis.

TIME:OUT

CHAPTER   ISAIAH   VERSE

40   30

"Even youths grow tired and weary, and young men stumble and fall; but those who hope in the Lord will renew their strength. They will soar on wings like eagles; they will run and not grow weary, they will walk and not be faint. " (NIV)

We may get exhausted on life's long road, but He renews our strength. And, one day, how awesome will it be when the Ruler of the Universe gives us the thumbs-up and ultimate reward for our X-treme faith?

CROSS TRAINING

BODY
Include some adventure in your vacations. Find a climbing wall, go snorkeling, run around the lake or along the beach, do a bike tour, go exploring, or go caving (with a guide). Even at home, you can investigate around where you live to see what good and healthy things you can get into.

SPIRIT
Take in the awesomeness of God's natural creation and beauty. Too often we take our surroundings for granted, and we forget to appreciate them. Look around where you live, work, and play; even a city park points out the art of God. Thank your creator for His wonderful creations and take a moment of contemplative prayer.

MIND
Write down and commit Isaiah 40: 30-31 to memory. Journal a few difficult challenges that are wearing you down. Whether it's sports, school, family, work, or just life, write a brief prayer beside each struggle. Ask God to renew your physical, mental, and spiritual strength.

_____

_____

_____

_____

_____

_____

_____

_____

_____

_____

_____

_____

_____

Fast Start

One of the greatest men of God I've ever had the privilege to meet was Bill Bright who I met while playing for Athletes in Action, the Sports Ministry of Campus Crusade for Christ. Bill, who is now with the Lord, founded Campus Crusade for Christ, a program that remains one of the most effective Christian ministries today. Bill was also awarded the Templeton Prize (think of winning the Heisman Trophy and NBA's Most Valuable Player for God). But it was one of Bill's books that truly inspired my Christian Brother and co-author, Win Davis, to fulfill the below verse of Matthew.

Bill wrote of his vision to have 2,000 Christians fast, only drinking liquids, for forty days. Win answered this call. As Win (a college and lifetime athlete) tells it, this call took more discipline than any athletic event he has ever trained for. It was a forty day marathon that challenged his body, mind, and Spirit. During his fast, Win only confided in a select group of Christians who supported him with prayer, encouragement, and freshly squeezed juices. Many of Win's friends, Christians and non-Christians alike, expressed concern over his rapid weight decline. They imagined he had cancer or another life-threatening disease. The only thing Win had, except for liquids, was the Holy Spirit and the prayers of other Christians to carry him through. And really, aren't those the only things we need?

TIME:OUT

CHAPTER

6

MATTHEW

VERSE

17

"But when you fast, be upbeat and wash your face, so that your fasting doesn't draw attention to you. Moreover your Father God will see your act in secret and will reward you." (NIV)

BODY

A proper diet is as important as exercise. For twenty-four hours, fast from processed foods (especially sweets). If you want to take this to the next level continue for a week, or even 21-40 days. Alternatively, choose one day each month to eat only fresh fruits, vegetables, nuts, and other healthy items.

SPIRIT

Commit this week to worship the Lord through giving, praying, and fasting. Take the first small step now by asking the Holy Spirit to guide you in these Spiritual Disciplines.

MIND

Read Matthew, chapter 6, in your bible. Journal some things you could sacrifice for God: some unhealthy food for 24 hours, some money to someone in need, or some time alone in prayer. Now go for it!

_____

_____

_____

_____

_____

_____

_____

_____

_____

_____

_____

_____

_____

Overcoming the Miss

If you are even a casual sports fan, you've probably heard of my college roommate. For over two decades the executives who put together the footage of previous Super Bowls' pivotal plays have chosen to highlight my college buddy. He is seen annually throughout the world because of missing the mark –literally. On January 27, 1991, with four seconds left in the game, Scott Norwood missed what would have been the winning field goal for who would have been the World Champion Buffalo Bills. The shame about "The Miss" has overshadowed the great things this All-Pro kicker did in the NFL. He broke O.J Simpson's scoring record, and, more importantly, raised thousands of dollars for children's charities.

As Christians, there will be times all of us fall short of people's expectations. And, despite our efforts, there will always be individuals who criticize our actions (especially those watching from the sidelines). The Bible is full of folks who followed God, and received far more jeers than cheers for their service. Jesus Christ endured this first hand, and He knew anyone who followed Him would be criticized and persecuted. He assured them that, in the end, they would be rewarded big time for their 'faith in action.' The key is to stay in the game and to keep on kicking. Tune out the negativity and listen to that affirming cheer within called The Holy Spirit.

TIME:OUT

CHAPTER JOHN **VERSE**

16   33

"In this world you will have trouble. But take heart! I have overcome the world." (NIV)

BODY

The biggest muscle in the human body is the quadriceps or thigh muscle. Swimming, soccer, cycling, running, karate, lifting, and even walking can strengthen this important muscle. So get moving!

SPIRIT

Pray for the strength and wisdom to handle the tough times. Then remember to always praise God for the good times.

MIND

Read John 16: 22-33. Journal about a time when things didn't work out the way you wanted. Write a few thoughts about how God could possibly use this struggle for both your growth and His glory.

_____

_____

_____

_____

_____

_____

_____

_____

_____

_____

_____

_____

_____

Just Do...Good!

One of the big differences between today's young athletes and when I played is that in most sports, there is now no off-season. With AAU, travel teams, year-round tournaments, meets and more, athletes seem to be getting less and less recovery time. They have less time to cross-train and less time to have a life outside of sports. It's easy to see how many athletes are staying injured, getting burned out quickly, or, worse, getting little exposure to the greatest coaching in the world (i.e. the Bible). One of the most disturbing trends is how 'Christian' students and parents are allowing sports to dictate their involvement in church and ministry.

The Apostle Paul encouraged the Galatian church to not grow weary of doing good, and assured them they would receive blessings for their efforts if they did not lose heart. It's important that we continue to "do good" for the Kingdom of God, which may mean voicing your opinion regarding the importance of spiritual time. You may not be able to change game times on Sunday, but you could offer suggestions such as incorporating a pre-game devotion or prayer. The key to success in *both* our sports life and our Spiritual life is training so that we will not grow weary or lose heart, so that we might "do good" when the competition (and competition for souls) is on the line.

TIME:OUT

CHAPTER GALATIANS **VERSE**

6 **9**

"And let us not grow weary while doing good, for in due season we shall reap if we do not lose heart." (NKJV)

CROSS TRAINING

BODY
Train so you won't grow weary. Set goals that go beyond your current limits. Do 10 more push ups, 10 more reps, 10 more minutes, or 10 more shots, (you get the picture).

SPIRIT
Brainstorm with friends to come up with innovative ways to include Christ in your activities. Gather players and parents to pray before games, host a pre-game meal and devotion, etc. Do good for God.

MIND
Read Galatians 6: 6-10. List the following; (1) Worshipping, (2) Spending time with Christian friends, (3) Going to Sunday school or Bible study, (4) Serving those less fortunate, (5) Sharing my faith in Jesus Christ. Now beside each one, grade yourself on how well you're doing. Journal how you can improve in each area and pray not to grow weary 'doing good.'

_____

_____

_____

_____

_____

_____

_____

_____

_____

_____

_____

_____

_____

When Teammates Disagree

My freshman year of college, I had a major disagreement with one of my teammates. He played offense while I played defense. He was very cocky, and his frequent trash talking caused more than one scuffle during practice. But despite our differences, and our sharp disagreements, both of us worked diligently toward our team's goal of playing in the conference championship – which we eventually did.

The Bible depicts several stories of disagreements, even among some of God's greatest followers. The Apostle Paul, who wrote most of the New Testament, occasionally scolds Christians in his letters to churches for focusing on their own selfish desires more that God's expectations of them. The Bible even tells us that Paul and his brother-in-Christ Barnabas got into such a disagreement that they went their separate ways. It's important to remember, however, that even though they disagreed, they kept their focus on serving Jesus Christ and doing His will.

Even today, Christians don't always see eye-to-eye on how to further God's kingdom. The important thing to remember is that it's OK for Christians to disagree on some things, as long as we don't lose our cool. However, we should never let those disagreements get in the way of our Christian team's goal. Together we need to share the Good News of Jesus Christ and work to serve as the hands and feet of one body – the body of our Lord and Savior, Jesus Christ.

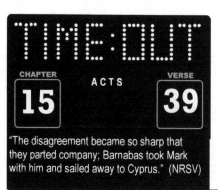

TIME·OUT

CHAPTER **ACTS** VERSE

15 **39**

"The disagreement became so sharp that they parted company; Barnabas took Mark with him and sailed away to Cyprus." (NRSV)

BODY

To become the best competitor you can be, you need to spend time working in all areas, even the ones you don't like. Whether it's giving it all in practice or doing drills and exercises you find monotonous, the key is to keep doing. Know it will all pay off for both you and the team.

SPIRIT

Pray for someone you've had a disagreement with. Ask God to allow you to forgive and reconcile with him or her.

MIND

Read about Paul and Barnabas in Acts, chapters 15. The Bible tells us they were effective Christians both together, and even after they disagreed. List a few people you've had disagreements with (e.g. parents, friends, boyfriends/girlfriends, teammates, etc). Journal how you still serve God, both in a team and individually.

_____

_____

_____

_____

_____

_____

_____

_____

_____

_____

_____

_____

_____

Athletes and Aliens

When talking about my college tennis days, I often joke about never losing a match...indoors. Although this is technically true, my winning streak isn't as impressive as it sounds. College tennis is primarily an outdoor sport, and few matches are played indoors. But the key to my indoor success was the dramatically different environment. The indoor courts where we practiced and played matches on during inclement weather had radically different lighting, playing surface, and humidity. Worse, it had an oven-like atmosphere that made exertion difficult. My opponents found these conditions uncomfortably different from the environment they were used to playing in. They were aliens on my 'tennis planet.'

The apostle Peter urges us not to get comfortable with the things of this world and not to give in to the sinful desires which "war against our soul." These desires can rob us of the potential God has for our lives. He urges us to realize that we are just temporary travelers and visitors during our time on earth. We are to be aliens and strangers so that even non-believers will see that there is something different about us. By living our lives in a Godly manner, we can preach without words. Non-believers can see the lights shining in us and accept the truth of God's amazing love.

TIME:OUT

CHAPTER **2** 1 PETER VERSE **11**

"Dear friends, I urge you, as aliens and strangers in the world, to abstain from sinful desires, which war against your soul." (NIV)

When we accept Jesus Christ as our Lord and Savior, we change from strangers to welcomed friends. We are to live lives that glorify God, and eventually He will reward us by taking us to our true home - Heaven.

CROSS TRAINING

BODY

Don't stop exercising just because of rain (or any other inclement weather for that matter). Have a workout plan prepared for those days you are stuck at home. If you don't have exercise equipment (treadmill, weights, etc.), you can get inexpensive equipment like rubber resistance tubes or return to classic exercises like pushups, sit-ups and stretching.

SPIRIT

Find a private room in your home, even if it's a closet, where you can spend some quiet time with just you and God.

MIND

Read 1 Peter 2: 9-12. Journal some steps you can take to glorify God by your actions. Write down a few things you will do this week to allow unbelievers to see how you are different because of what Christ has done in your life.

_____

_____

_____

_____

_____

_____

_____

_____

_____

_____

_____

_____

_____

Supernatural Strength Training

Every athlete goes through 'slumps,' those times when their performance falls considerably short of their ability. Despite hours and hours of training and practice, they just can't make a basket, land a first serve in, hit a ball, throw straight, or kick accurately. They feel as if they have been zapped of their talent, energy, stamina, and strength. The key to overcoming a slump is to believe in yourself, push yourself forward, and continue your training. Otherwise, you may only get weaker and make your slump last longer.

The same holds true of the Christian walk. There will be Spiritual slumps and valleys when your faith feels weak. There will be times you can't feel the presence of God. "I can do all things through Christ who strengthens me" was one of the first Bible verses I committed to memory. I needed something practical that I could understand, and I wanted a verse that would give me encouragement when I lost confidence or felt discouraged.

There are going to be times in your life when you will experience self-doubt, and there will be times people will tell you that you can't or won't accomplish your goals. Remove the word "can't" from your vocabulary. Know that beyond a shadow of a doubt God is with you, and He will never leave you. His Holy Spirit and words live in you.

TIME:OUT

CHAPTER **PHILIPPIANS** VERSE

4 **13**

"I can do all things through Christ who strengthens me." (NKJV)

CROSS TRAINING

BODY
The best way to prepare for slumps are to prepare in advance. Improve your conditioning, strength and skills a little bit more each week. Visualize your successful performance constantly in your mind and keep pressing forward knowing that you can do all things through Christ who gives you strength.

SPIRIT
Ask God for the strength to endure life's slumps and challenges. Pray for the Holy Spirit to help you understand how to rejoice in the Lord even during the tough times.

MIND
Read Philippians chapter 4. In this God-inspired letter, the Apostle Paul writes some very encouraging words to followers of Christ. Journal how Christ gives you strength and as Paul writes, "Rejoice in the Lord - Always!"

_____

_____

_____

_____

_____

_____

_____

_____

_____

_____

_____

_____

_____

Don't Slack Off

One of the most exhilarating moments in sports is 'The Goal Line Stand.' Here, as little as an inch separates the opposing offense from scoring a touchdown. When playing defense, a team needs every bit of skill and heart to successfully hold off the opposition. Not a single player can afford to slack off. Refusing to give an inch can be the difference between winning or losing a game, or even a championship.

The Apostle Paul gives some great advice to his young disciple, Timothy. I especially love 1 Timothy 6:13 (the Message version). Here, Paul urges Timothy to follow in Christ's example, "Keep this command to the letter, and don't slack off." Notice that this interpretation says Jesus didn't give an inch once he took the stand. When it comes to our Christian faith, we are not to give a centimeter to the opposition. Paul instructed Timothy not to let others water down the teachings of God's Holy Word. Some things are non-negotiable.

God loves us so much that he didn't want us to spend eternity apart from Him. But the only way to join our Father is through Jesus. Therefore, we must confess our sins and accept Jesus Christ as our Lord and Savior to enter His Kingdom of Heaven. We must tap into the practice, perseverance, and passion that has prepared us to follow Christ. Prepare to hold your ground by reading, meditating, proclaiming, and living God's Holy Word.

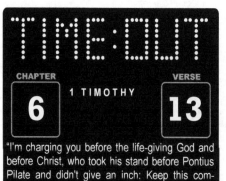

TIME·OUT

CHAPTER — 1 TIMOTHY — VERSE
6 **13**

"I'm charging you before the life-giving God and before Christ, who took his stand before Pontius Pilate and didn't give an inch: Keep this command to the letter, and don't slack off. Our Master, Jesus Christ, is on his way. " (MSG)

BODY

Improve inch by inch and don't slack off! In other words, don't wait until the season is upon you to be ready. Improve your conditioning, strength and skills a little bit more each week. Don't slack off and think you can make up your neglect quickly – You can't so just do it! – Now!

SPIRIT

Thank God for the encouragement in His Word. Pray that the Holy Spirit will give you the courage to face any opposition to proclaiming Jesus Christ in both your words and actions. Ask God to keep you from giving an inch and to move forward.

MIND

Read 1 Timothy 6: 11-21. Imagine the Apostle Paul is personally giving you these instructions. Journal a few ways you can immediately apply Paul's coaching to your life. In what areas do you need to stop slacking off and make a stand?

_____

_____

_____

_____

_____

_____

_____

_____

_____

_____

_____

_____

_____

Faith Reps

One of the ways colleges and professional scouts evaluate strength is observing the number of times an athlete can lift a certain weight. They know that repetition (bench pressing 225 pounds as many times as possible, for example) is a much better indicator of strength than a one-time "max" lift. Repeating the lift shows endurance, the type of strength that will be needed to last an entire game and a long season.

Moses had a similar philosophy for strengthening the faith of God's people. He told them to commit themselves to God's instruction by learning God's commands by heart, and then committing themselves wholeheartedly to obeying those commands. He assured them, that by doing so, the Lord would bless them.

Repeating God's commands and meditating on them over and over again (especially within a family) is the most effective way to make them part of your faith walk. Meeting and praying regularly with your family, friends, church, and teammates is far more effective than a one-time super sermon, inspirational speech, youth rally, Christian camp, etc. Those are all good, but the best way to build long-lasting Spiritual strength is by getting in your 'Faith Reps' everyday. Read God's Word (the Bible) over and over and over again. Then 'put into play' what you've learned in both your words and actions!

TIME:OUT

CHAPTER **6** DEUTERONOMY VERSE **7**

"Repeat them (God's commands) again and again to your children. Talk about them when you are at home and when you are away on a journey, when you are lying down and when you are getting up again." (NLT)

BODY

It's "old school," but doing 3 sets of 10-12 reps with weights for every muscle group is still one of the best ways to increase overall strength and muscle endurance.

SPIRIT

Ask your family to read the Bible and/or do a devotion together (perhaps this one or others from *Cross-Training*). Pray aloud – "Lord, show us how to love you with all our heart, soul and might."

MIND

Read Deuteronomy 6: 1-9. Journal the ways you show your love to God with all your heart, soul and might. Is it a long list or a short list? Think about it!

_____

_____

_____

_____

_____

_____

_____

_____

_____

_____

_____

_____

Anger Makes for Losers

One of the most bizarre events in sports, I've ever been involved in was during my freshman year as a college football player. Our team was leading 21-7 against our bitter in-state conference rival when a bench-clearing brawl broke out between the two teams. The officials weren't able to control the melee and stopped the game in the third quarter. Despite the fact we were winning the game, both teams were given a loss. That day we were losers because all the hard work and effort we put into being our best was forfeited because of our team's inability to keep our cool.

Jesus was fully aware of the damage anger could do in one's life. He said that if we lose our cool and insult our brothers and sisters-in-Christ, then we are guilty of sin. He said that we shouldn't even come to the Lord with our offering until we've set things straight with those who we're fighting or arguing with. Jesus even said that if we lose our cool in anger, then we are subject to the same type of judgment which falls on a murderer.

How about you? Is there anyone you're constantly arguing or fighting with? Do you struggle with anger? Jesus said that if we forgive others, God will forgive us,. But if we do not forgive others, God will not forgive us. Commit this day to forgiving someone who you're mad at. Talk to a pastor or counselor if your anger is getting the best of you. Ask God to help you control your anger.

TIME:OUT

CHAPTER — MATTHEW — VERSE

5   **21**

'You have heard that the law of Moses says, "Do not murder. If you commit murder, you are subject to judgment." But I say, if you are angry with someone, you are subject to judgment!" ' (NLT)

BODY

Convert your negative emotions into positive physical conditioning. Use exercise as a release as you attack your workout (not your opponent). Pound a heavy bag or other piece of martial arts/boxing equipment. Use your strong emotions to get stronger – get in one more lap or rep in the weight room. Turn your negative energy into positive results.

SPIRIT

Ask God's forgiveness for the times you've lost your cool. Ask someone you've angered for forgiveness. Forgive someone who has angered you. Ask someone who you trust if you have an anger problem. If so, seek Christian counseling lest your anger hurts others and subjects you to the Lord's judgment.

MIND

Note Read Matthew 5:21-26. List the names of those you are having disagreements with. Journal the steps 'you' will take to resolve those disputes.

_____

_____

_____

_____

_____

_____

_____

_____

_____

_____

_____

_____

The Truly Gifted Athlete

I always wanted to be a major college basketball player, and I have shot baskets for as long as I can remember. When I was a kid on a small farm, my best buddy, Steve, and I actually nailed the metal hoop from a broken barrel to the side of a barn (No James Naismith jokes. I'm not that old and besides that was a peach basket). Through all this practice, I got pretty good. I made the starting line-up on my high school basketball team, and I was named co-captain my senior year. But unlike my Christian brother and co-author, Calvin Duncan, who was an All-American in both high school and college, I didn't have the God-given talent to play at the next level. I was a six-foot, 200-pound power forward with a lot of heart—and no recruiters. What little talent I had, plus my heart, did get the attention of a few football coaches. I ended up signing a scholarship to play a sport that was more suited to the gifts God had given me.

The Apostle Paul wrote that each of us have different spiritual gifts, according to God's will and grace. Some of those gifts include teaching, encouraging, leading, coaching, etc. But they also include things such as serving, sharing, and giving (something we can all do). Paul wrote that God made us all unique so that we can use our special talents to work together as one great team (making up what Paul calls the body of Christ). The truly gifted athlete uses his God-given talents to give his very best to his Christian teammates and, most importantly, to God.

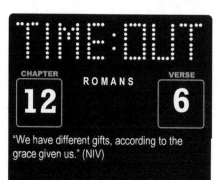

TIME·OUT

CHAPTER **ROMANS** VERSE

12 **6**

"We have different gifts, according to the grace given us." (NIV)

BODY

Core training is essential in developing all athletic talent. Strengthening your mid-section enhances ability and increases endurance. Get with a coach or trainer and work your core and improve upon the natural gifts God has given you.

SPIRIT

Pray about your Spiritual gifts and begin applying the talents God has given you to serve your church, small group and especially in the unbelieving world around you. Ask God to provide opportunities for you to use your talent to proclaim the Good News of Jesus Christ in both words and actions.

MIND

Read Romans 12: 1 - 8. Write down a few talents God has given you. See if your church has a Spiritual gifts test or find one at a local Christian bookstore. Ask a mature Christian to help you identify your gifts. You may be surprised to see what God has gifted you with to further His kingdom.

His Punishment Fit Our Crime

Every sport has some form of disciplinary action for poor choices, unacceptable behavior, and/or attitudes. I must admit I got what I deserved a few times as a young athlete. I had to run the stadium steps when I arrived late for football practice. When I blew a move in karate, I had to do extra pushups. And, following a poor team effort in either basketball or tennis, my teammates and I lined up for the classic spots' torture – suicides (which entail sprinting from line to line dozens of times).

The Bible tells us of a man who was truly tortured, but who believed his punishment was well deserved. We don't know his name, only that he was nailed to a criminal's cross beside Jesus at the Crucifixion. The Bible records that this man defended Jesus when another criminal began to taunt Him. He told the criminal, "We are being punished justly and getting what we deserved, but this man (Jesus) has done nothing wrong." After confessing his sins, the criminal asked Jesus to remember him when He ascended to Heaven. Jesus knew that this sinner had truly repented. He told him, "Today you will be with me in paradise." Our sins may not be as bad (in our eyes) as the criminal's, but they are sins nevertheless. They must be forgiven by the One who died for us – Jesus Christ. Ask Jesus for forgiveness and guidance. Trust that He will show you the way to Heaven.

TIME:OUT

CHAPTER 23   LUKE   **VERSE** 41

"We are punished justly, for we are getting what our deeds deserve. But this man has done nothing wrong." (NIV)

BODY

Learning from your mistakes can be beneficial, if you accept your punishment as a learning experience. Later in my training I actually incorporated the exercises I had originally been given as punishment. Running up stairs, doing extra pushups and even suicides will dramatically improve your conditioning.

Ask God to forgive you for the things that displease Him. Thank Jesus for His willingness to die for those sins, and if you haven't already, pray to accept Jesus Christ as Lord & Savior.

SPIRIT

MIND

Read Luke 23: 26-55 (and chapter 24) for the most powerful story in the Bible. List those sins in your life that Jesus died for and journal some ways you can avoid situations that could get in the way of the awesome plan God has for your life.

_____

_____

_____

_____

_____

_____

_____

_____

_____

_____

_____

_____

_____

His Pain, Our Gain

My personal trainer, Vernon, is one determined guy. Even when he was a kid, he dreamed of playing big time college football. But throughout his life, he's gone through many things that would make most people quit. When he was in high school, he suffered a stroke. The right side of his body was paralyzed, and he had no speech. He missed six months of school, and he had to attend a military academy to make up his grades so that he could go to college. He finally received a scholarship to play for Virginia Tech, one of the premier college football programs in the country. He then suffered a career ending shoulder injury. He never gave up, and now God is using his determination and sacrifice to help others. He instills the importance of physical fitness and good nutrition to all types of people, including at-risk kids, athletes, and even old guys like me.

Shortly before He was about to be crucified, Jesus told his closest friends that He would have to suffer and ultimately die. Even His friend Peter tried to talk Him out of it, but Jesus told Peter that he needed to focus on God and not the world. He explained that people could gain the whole world and still lose their eternal soul. It's important to remember that Jesus chose to suffer excruciating pain and sacrifice, even though he could have avoided it. He did this so that all types of people, including you and I, would not have to suffer eternally, but one day could spend eternity in Heaven!

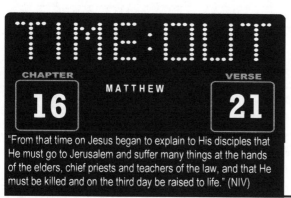

TIME:OUT

CHAPTER

MATTHEW

16

VERSE

21

"From that time on Jesus began to explain to His disciples that He must go to Jerusalem and suffer many things at the hands of the elders, chief priests and teachers of the law, and that He must be killed and on the third day be raised to life." (NIV)

BODY

Suffering a little discomfort by pushing yourself a little harder can make a big difference. I was not the best athlete on my team, but I was determined to go to college and giving my all in sports helped make that dream come true. Push yourself to the top of your game, and maximum potential.

SPIRIT

Be careful not to push God away by pushing (or being pushed) away from church, Bible study, serving those in need, etc. to play sports. God first!

MIND

Read Matthew 16: 13-28. Journal some things that may seem good in the world, but can take your focus off serving Jesus Christ. Write how you can include God in those things.

_____

_____

_____

_____

_____

_____

_____

_____

_____

_____

_____

_____

_____

_____

_____

Be A Leader...Serve Others

You may never have heard of Don Meyer, Head Coach for Northern State University, despite the fact that he has won a National Championship and more games (over 900) than any other men's college basketball coach in history. Coach Meyer's dedication to his players is legendary. He coached in a wheelchair after losing his leg in a car accident, and he continued to coach despite having inoperable cancer. One of the most powerful things I heard Coach Meyer say was, "If you're a leader and you're not a servant leader, then you're not a leader." He notes a lot of people want to be leaders, but they are not willing to be servants. He also stresses the importance of doing something good with each day God has given him.

The Apostle Peter urged us to serve with the gifts we received from God, and he stressed that our service must be done with the strength God gives us (so no slacking off or half-effort). We are to look for opportunities to serve. We are to use those opportunities and the gifts we have received to praise God by serving in the name of Jesus Christ. Finally, we are to serve one another with love, because, as Peter wrote, love covers many sins. What are your gifts? Are you looking for opportunities to use those gifts? Commit to serving in the name of the One who loved you so much, He gave His very life to cover your sins. Be a great leader and be an example. Serve others.

TIME:OUT

CHAPTER **4**   1 PETER   VERSE **10**

"Each one should use whatever gift he has received to serve others, faithfully administering God's grace in its various forms." (NIV)

BODY

Sports camps & clinics are some of the best ways to improve your game and abilities. Ask coaches and others to recommend a few and let them know if money is an issue. There are many inexpensive local camps & clinics, and many offer need-based scholarships. If you are blessed with any athletic gifts, look into serving at a camp or clinic. You'll be blessed serving others.

SPIRIT

Pray for God to reveal the gifts He has given you and how to use those talents to acknowledge him, giving praise to Christ Jesus.

MIND

Read 1 Peter 4: 7-19. Journal some of your talents & gifts. Now write some ways you can use those gifts to bring glory to God by being a servant leader.

_____

_____

_____

_____

_____

_____

_____

_____

_____

_____

_____

_____

Do the Right Thing Even When It's Uncomfortable

When I was a young writer living in Atlanta, the University of Georgia received negative national press when they fired a professor named Jan Kemp. She had revealed that the university's athletes were given preferential treatment in the classroom, and many had failed to meet even the minimal test scores required for college admission. Professor Kemp was persecuted and harshly criticized for courageously telling the truth (though she was later given her job back and awarded over a million dollars in damages for this injustice). Kemp's bold truth led to many changes in college athletics, and, in the long run, helped athletes get a valid education instead of just being used for their athletic ability. Before the changes, many athletes who didn't make it to the professional level left college with no degree, and little hope of finding a good job.

Jesus Christ, in his most famous sermon, said that Christians will be blessed for being persecuted and standing up for what's right and just in God's sight. They will receive the Kingdom of Heaven. Don't back down from boldly telling the truth, especially the Good News. God sent His son, Jesus Christ, into the world to save all of us from our sins, and now we can spend eternity in Heaven. Remember that when you do the right thing, even when it's uncomfortable, you will be blessed in the long run, especially when you graduate from this life to the next.

TIME:OUT

CHAPTER **MATTHEW** VERSE

5 **10**

"Blessed are those of you who are persecuted for doing what's just and right in God's sight." (Int.)

CROSS TRAINING

BODY
Success in sports takes both body "and" mind. Keep up in the classroom to stay mentally strong. Study your playbook and read up on the best and latest athletic techniques and training, but also stay on top of your math, science, English and other subjects that will help you long after your playing days are over.

SPIRIT
Pray for boldness to tell others what is just and right, even if it's not the popular thing to do.

MIND
Read a few versions of Matthew 5:1-12 and strive to understand what each of the Beatitudes mean in your life (ask your pastor, Sunday School teacher or Christian friend to help you). Journal how you can display these characteristics in your life.

_____

_____

_____

_____

_____

_____

_____

_____

_____

_____

_____

_____

_____

The Highest Award is Respect

While we were writing this sport's devotional, the sports world suffered back-to-back-to-back black eyes. First, the most decorated athlete in Olympic history was caught on camera smoking marijuana. Shortly thereafter, arguably the best player in professional baseball admitted to using performance-enhancing drugs after the story broke in a popular sports magazine. And Finally, *Sports Illustrated* magazine's Male Athlete of the Decade, and one of the most respected family men in sports, admitted to adultery after reports of his numerous extramarital affairs were published following weeks of rumors and speculation. Sports talk shows and news programs around the world have reported on the millions of dollars these athletes will lose in endorsement deals because the good names of these once revered athletes are tarnished forever.

The writer of Proverbs reports that one's reputation is more valuable than wealth, and respect is worth more than silver or gold. What's your reputation? What do your actions and attitude say about you? How does your behavior influence the way others perceive you in school, at work, and on the field of play? Have you earned the respect of your peers and leaders? Ask yourself this question, "when it comes to drawing others closer to Jesus Christ, am I an attraction or a distraction?" If the answer is not "an attraction," it's time to work on your good name. A good reputation is even more important than your game.

TIME·OUT

CHAPTER **22**   PROVERBS   VERSE **1**

"A good name is more desirable than great riches; to be esteemed is better than silver or gold." (NIV)

CROSS TRAINING

BODY
The way to get respect and a good reputation, as an athlete, is the earn it. The greatest leaders lead by example. They give everything they've got. They don't give up in the face of adversity, and they don't cheat. True leaders are respected at a game's end, regardless of the score.

SPIRIT
Pray for God's Spirit to direct your actions, so that your reputation can speak louder than words. Earn the respect of others, and pray to be God's attraction, not God's distraction.

MIND
Read the great wisdom of Proverbs 22:1-16. Draw a line down the center of your journal. On one side write how you can be an attraction to God (i.e. draw others nearer to Him). On the other side, write how you can be a distraction from God (words and actions that could get in the way of your service). Place a big X on the distraction side, and strive daily to move yourself towards God.

_____

_____

_____

_____

_____

_____

_____

_____

_____

_____

_____

_____

_____

Just Think Just Thoughts

While in Chicago, I met (and had my picture taken with) one of my childhood heroes, Gale Sayers. Gale was an All-Pro Running back for the Chicago Bears, and he is still regarded as one of the best return men ever to play in the NFL. His six touchdowns in a single game still stands atop the record books. But Gale also inspired me with his courage, loyalty, and friendship to his dying friend and teammate, Brian Piccolo. Gale, who is black, showed his love for Brian, who was white, during a time of open racial prejudice in America. This friendship inspired the movie *Brian's Song,* and Gale's book *I Am Third* was the first sports book I ever read (by the way, Gale notes "The Lord is first."). Gale said that one of the reasons for his success was that, before he ever touched the ball, he would envision the play. He would actually see himself making those sweet moves to avoid would-be tacklers.

The Apostle Paul wrote that Christians should fill our heads with positive thoughts about things that are true, noble, just, pure, lovely, admirable, outstanding, and praiseworthy. He told his followers that if they followed their coaching, then surely the God of peace would be them. If we think about God's instructions before our next move, our walk with the Lord and potential for an awesome life can be, like Gale's moves, "sweet!"

TIME:OUT

CHAPTER   PHILIPPIANS   VERSE

4   **8**

"In closing my dear brothers and sisters in Christ, whatever is true, noble, just, pure, lovely or admirable; if anything is excellent or praiseworthy – think about such things." (ILNT)

CROSS TRAINING

BODY
Play out successful performances in your mind to improve your game and athletic success. Visualize the foul shot going in, the perfect stroke, kick, throw, run, etc. See, believe & achieve.

SPIRIT
Ask God to show you the positive potential of people that are challenging you. Try to find one true, noble, just, pure, lovely, admirable, excellent or praiseworthy thing to say to them. It might just change their heart...and yours.

MIND
Read Philippians 4:1-9. Journal a few things/people who have you anxious and concerned. Write a short prayer by each asking God to help you cope and direct your next steps. Visualize and describe the good that could come from the situations.

_____

_____

_____

_____

_____

_____

_____

_____

_____

_____

_____

_____

_____

_____

Encourage Each Other

"What did you do? Fall off the bench?" Three decades have passed, but I can still feel the sting of that coach's negative comment. It was my first year playing on my first team sport for my school. I had worked hard all summer to get myself in shape. But shortly after the season began, I developed a common, albeit painful condition, among young growing athletes called Osgood-Schlatters Disease. My pediatrician told my mom and me that I needed to stop playing sports for a while. I remember feeling terrible about not playing, but this paled in comparison to the hurt and humiliation I felt from the coach's cutting words. I had gone up to him after practice in the first couple weeks, and I told him that I was injured and could no longer play. The coach laughed, and then asked me if I'd fallen off the bench. As a young athlete who just wanted to be part of the team, I needed encouragement. But this discouragement left me hurt and angry.

When the Apostle Paul was coaching his new (Christian) team in Thessalonica, he called them names like "Beloved," "Children of the Light," "Brother," and "Sister." He inspired them by telling them that they were protected by faith and love. He instructed them to go forth with the confidence of their salvation. God had destined them for success in their faith. He finished by saying, "May the grace of our Lord Jesus Christ be with you." With positive and encouraging words like that, his team was no doubt motivated to go out and give it their best.

TIME:OUT

CHAPTER **5**   FIRST THESSALONIANS   VERSE **11**

"Therefore encourage one another and build each other up, just as in fact you are doing." (NIV)

BODY

You can't always control what others say to you, but you can control the way you react. Use negative remarks and questions about your ability to motivate you to be the best you can be. Two years after that coach's comments, I worked my tail off and became his leading scorer.

SPIRIT

Pray that the Holy Spirit would help you be an encourager and not discourager of people.

MIND

Read 1 Thessalonians Chapter 5. In your journal, write the names of 3 people you interact with regularly. Write something positive about each and commit to encouraging each person this week.

_____
_____
_____
_____
_____
_____
_____
_____
_____
_____
_____
_____
_____

Just Do...for Others

My high school coach, Bob Myers, and I have been friends for over twenty-five years . Coach Myers was both my head football and track coach. He appointed me co-captain of the football team my senior year. He invested extra hours to help me hone my skills, and he played an essential role in helping me attend college on an athletic scholarship. As my physical education teacher, he also taught me about the importance of life-long exercise and nutrition. Several years later, God blessed me to be in a position to say thanks to Coach Myers (who had been promoted to Athletic Director) by providing scholarships to help other student athletes go to college.

In what has become known as 'The Golden Rule,' Jesus said, "Do for others what you would like them to do for you." He explained that this simple statement basically summed up everything the Bible and great prophets taught. Later, in the Gospel of Matthew, Jesus drove this point home. He told the people around Him that the greatest commandment is to love the Lord God with all their hearts, souls, and minds. And the second most important commandment is to love their neighbors as themselves.

In summary, Jesus stated that the teaching of the Bible and words of the prophets are based on the idea that we show our love for God by loving, doing, and caring for others as much as ourselves. As followers of Jesus Christ, it's important to invest our time in helping others who could use a little (or a lot) of help.

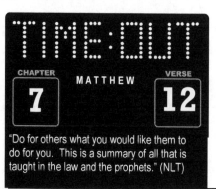

TIME:OUT

CHAPTER
7

MATTHEW

VERSE
12

"Do for others what you would like them to do for you. This is a summary of all that is taught in the law and the prophets." (NLT)

CROSS TRAINING

BODY

Do for your body what you want it to do for you. In other words, if you want it to perform a certain skill during competition, you must practice that skill over and over again. If you want it to stay "stronger for longer" you must push yourself consistently during practice and on your own.

SPIRIT

Jesus gave His life for our sins. If you haven't accepted Christ as Savior and asked Him to forgive your sins, do it now so that you can spend eternity in Heaven with God. If you have accepted Him, follow Christ by doing for others what you would like for them to do for you.

MIND

Read Matthew 7: 1-12. Note how Jesus teaches us how to treat others. Journal a few times you have judged others and/or treated others differently than you would want to be treated. Now journal how you can (and will) do better!

_____

_____

_____

_____

_____

_____

_____

_____

_____

_____

_____

_____

Game Film

One of the things that helped me earn a scholarship to play college ball was my game film. The good and bad thing about being filmed is that every move you make, or don't make, is caught on tape. The visual evidence of your actions and inactions are in plain sight, and they are watched over and over again by those evaluating you. They observe when you hustle and when you slack off, when you make a great play and when you blow your assignment, when you play within the rules or when you try to get around them, when you succeed and when you fail. Usually the coaches and players pick out the best games to send out, ones which highlight an athlete's talent and potential to play at the next level.

The Apostle Paul strongly urged the church in Corinth to be careful about judging the faith and actions of others, then he noted that the Lord knows our deepest secrets and motives. He knows if we are focused on selfish motives or if we have made Him our Lord and Savior. He observes every action we take, or don't take. Unlike game film, we don't get to pick and choose which of our actions God sees. He sees our behavior 24/7, so let's make sure pleasing God is our # 1 priority. We will make mistakes along the way, but God sees into our hearts and knows our intentions. Let's focus on creating a 'human highlight film' that will glorify God and let him know we are ready for the next level.

TIME:OUT

CHAPTER | FIRST CORINTHIANS | VERSE
4 | FIRST CORINTHIANS | **5**

"So be careful not to jump to conclusions before the Lord returns as to whether or not someone is faithful. When the Lord comes, he will bring our deepest secrets to light and will reveal our private motives. And then God will give to everyone whatever praise is due." (NLT)

CROSS TRAINING

BODY

Play and practice as though all your efforts are being videotaped. Go all out! Often, someone is watching your actions and attitude on the court (or any field of play) and off.

SPIRIT

Confess your deepest secrets and selfish motives to God. Ask for forgiveness for the times you've failed to be Christ-like in your words and actions, and pray for the Holy Spirit's guidance to help strengthen your faith and service to God.

MIND

Read 1 Corinthians 4: 1-5. Journal a time recently when your selfish motives got in the way of your service to Christ. Write out how you can (and will) change that.

_____

_____

_____

_____

_____

_____

_____

_____

_____

_____

_____

_____

_____

_____

Faith Hall of Fame

One of the most memorable experiences of my basketball career was being invited to try out for the American National Team, a team that would later compete at the Pan American Games. There, at the Olympic Training Center in Colorado Springs, Colorado, I competed against the very best in the world – literally a Who's Who of Hoops. Michael Jordan, Charles Barkley, Karl Malone, John Stockton, and other NBA stars were all there. I had to have faith in myself just to compete, and I gave everything I had to be noticed among players who would one day be in the Basketball Hall of Fame.

Hebrews 11 is often referred to as the "Faith Hall of Fame." It's literally a Who's Who of Heavenly Heroes who came before Jesus Christ. Abraham, Noah, Moses, David and other Biblical All-Starts are listed, as well as many others who gave their lives for God. But do you know what's most exciting about the people on this list? One day you could be invited to join this chosen group. The invitation will not be based on your earthly talent that fades with time, but on your faith in Jesus Christ which leads to eternal life. Are you giving your best to God? How awesome will it be one day to hear Jesus say, "Well done, good and faithful servant. You made the team!"

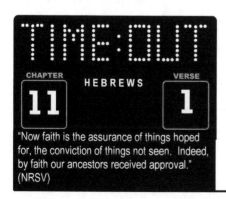

TIME·OUT

CHAPTER **HEBREWS** VERSE

11 **1**

"Now faith is the assurance of things hoped for, the conviction of things not seen. Indeed, by faith our ancestors received approval."
(NRSV)

CROSS TRAINING

BODY

To be the best you must compete against the best. As a former college and pro coach, I can tell you the guy who wants to go up against the best player will not only make himself/herself better, but he or she will also get the coach's attention quickly.

SPIRIT

Download the song "Lazarus Come Forth" by Carmen. Listen to the song while looking at the lyrics, then close your eyes and listen to the song again. Meditate on what it would be like in the midst of this Faith Hall of Fame. Thank God that one day you will be there if you accept and follow the Way of Jesus Christ.

MIND

Read all of Hebrews Chapter 11. Journal what you would like God to say about your faith walk e.g. "By faith, (insert your name) boldly ... (You get the idea).

It Takes Teamwork to Make the Dream Work

"It takes teamwork to make the dream work." If it were up to me, that would have been the slogan for both the 1992 Olympic Basketball "Dream Team" and 2008 "Redeem Team." I had the privilege to experience the former first-hand when a few other All-Americans and I were invited to compete against the members of "The Dream Team." What made those superstars, and the ones on the 2008 Olympic squad, gold medalists was, despite their great individual talent, each committed to putting the team ahead of themselves. This was especially true for the 2008 squad whose individuals had to put every bit of their heart into working together as a team to compete against their international opponents who had kept the Americans from winning the Gold Medal in the previous Olympics.

In Scripture, Nehemiah was God's point man, and had put it on Nehemiah's heart to rebuild Jerusalem's wall. The challenge was that the opponents of God's people planned on keeping the wall from being built. It would take a team effort to both rebuild Jerusalem's wall and protect God's people from their enemies at the same time. But that's just what God's people did because *"they had a heart for the work"* – God's work that is. When Christians work together, we are building God's Kingdom, and often we get blessed in the process. Remember the acronym *T.E.A.M.S* - **T**ogether **E**veryone **A**chieves **M**ore **S**uccess.

TIME:OUT

CHAPTER

4

NEHEMIAH

VERSE

6

"We kept at it, repairing and rebuilding the wall. The whole wall was soon joined together and halfway to its intended height because the people had a heart for the work." (MSG)

CROSS TRAINING

BODY

Team Tag is a great conditioning game for all sports. It's like regular tag except each time a person gets tagged they have to lock hands, and work as a team to capture the free players. Have fun and get fit at the same time.

SPIRIT

Go as a team of believers to a specific place and pray for God's intervention. Pray as you stand in your school, athletic field, workplace, neighborhood, etc.

MIND

Read Nehemiah 4. Note how together God's people rebuilt the wall of Jerusalem. Write down the name of some Christian friends. List their strengths and journal what you could do together to proclaim and build up the name of God.

_____

_____

_____

_____

_____

_____

_____

_____

_____

_____

_____

_____

_____

Step Up to the Next Level

One brother-in-Christ I've had the privilege to compete and coach against is Mike Davis. That name might sound familiar. Mike received national attention when he succeeded Bobby Knight (one of the most successful coaches in NCAA Men's basketball history) as head coach for Indiana University. Many thought Mike would never measure up to his mentor, but in his first season he won more games than any first-year coach in IU's history. And he was the only IU coach to begin his head coaching career with three straight 20-plus win seasons and three straight NCAA Tournament appearances. He was chosen as the National Coach of the Year, and he led his team to college basketball's "promise land"– the NCAA Final Four (where he led the Indiana Hoosiers to the National Championship game).

The Bible tells us of another man who had even bigger shoes to fill. His name was Joshua, and he had served under Moses, the greatest man-of-God in the history of Israel at that time. After Moses led God's people on a forty year journey through the wilderness, God chose Joshua to succeed Moses and lead His people to "The Promised Land." The Bible says the Lord told Joshua to be bold and courageous. He told Joshua that He would be with him as he led God's people. As Christians, we are called to be bold and courageous regarding our faith in Jesus Christ. Are you following God's direction, or do you risk wandering in the wilderness of this world?

TIME:OUT

CHAPTER **DEUTERONOMY** VERSE

31   **23**

"Be strong and courageous, for you will bring the Israelites into the land I promised them on oath, and I myself will be with you." (NIV)

CROSS TRAINING

BODY

Coaches can help take your game to the next level. Schedule a one-on-one meeting with your coach and ask what kind of physical drills and mental preparations you can do to improve your game and be an asset to the team.

SPIRIT

Mike Davis received both praise and criticism because his teams didn't practice on Sundays. It was a bold statement of his faith. Pray for boldness and the courage to put God before all things – including sports.

MIND

Read Deuteronomy 31: 14-30. This is a powerful story of how God disciplines us when we turn our backs on Him. Listen to the 'Spiritual coaches' God has placed for you on earth. Is God your God or are sports (or something else) your God? Journal those things that threaten to take the place of God, and list how you will put God above all things.

_____

_____

_____

_____

_____

_____

_____

_____

_____

_____

_____

_____

_____

Playing Both Halves for Jesus

Imagine playing the first-half of a game flawlessly. Can you picture yourself playing completely 'in the zone'? Sure. Maybe you've even been fortunate enough to make this dream a reality. Almost every shot was a winner. Every play was executed to perfection. Every bounce bounced your way, and every call was made in your favor. But what if you decided that your success was enough, even if you hadn't completed the game? You believed your efforts during the first-half entitled you to the win, so you decided to declare victory without finishing the game? "No way!" your opponent would protest. The game is not over until *both* halves have been played.

If we're not careful, even Christians can be just as misguided. "If we're saved by God's grace," some seem to think, "then works aren't important." They spend the rest of their lives on the sidelines watching the game. But the Bible is very clear that both halves - faith and works are important. The Apostle Paul said that we are saved by grace so that we don't go around boasting, but we were created to do good works for Christ Jesus. The half-brother of Jesus, James, said that faith without works is dead. Even Jesus told His followers that those who neglected the less fortunate would not enter the Kingdom of Heaven. Jesus died on the cross for your sins to give you the amazing gift of salvation. We need to both accept his gift, and serve those that Jesus called "the least of these."

TIME:OUT

CHAPTER		VERSE
2	EPHESIANS	**8**

"For by grace you have been saved through faith, and this is not your own doing; it is the gift of God-- not the result of works, so that no one may boast. For we are what he has made us, created in Christ Jesus for good works, which God prepared beforehand to be our way of life." (NRSV)

CROSS TRAINING

BODY
Which is more important - cardio or strength training? Trick question - both! Get with your coach or your trainer, and make sure you have a workout designed to develop both stamina and strength.

SPIRIT
During your quiet time this week, pray for opportunities to both 'do good works' and to share the 'Good News' that God gives us all the gift of eternal life through faith in Jesus Christ.

MIND
Read Ephesians 2: 4-10 and Matthew 25: 31-46. Note how perfectly faith and works fit together. Have you accepted God's grace through His Son Jesus Christ? If you have, are you serving Christ by serving those less fortunate? Journal how you can (and will) play *both* halves this week for Jesus Christ.

_____

_____

_____

_____

_____

_____

_____

_____

_____

_____

_____

_____

_____

Fully Charged

As I look around the coliseum, one thing that has changed over the years since I played college and pro ball is that almost everyone owns a cell phone or PDA (Personal Digital Assistant). During every timeout, intermission, halftime, or other break, everyone is talking, texting, taking pictures, and/or checking their e-mails. Sometimes, even during the game I'll spot someone taking a video to post online and/or on one of the many social networking sites. After the game, when everyone gets home, most have another thing in common – they need to recharge their electronic gadgets so they will continue to operate at full capacity.

There's another and better way to recharge. Depend on the Lord; He gives us enough strength to operate at full capacity. His "power" can help us deal with our issues on a daily basis. He can get us through discouragements, temptations, poor choices, and other things that drain us. His power is greater than drugs, alcohol, tobacco, sex, popularity, and even shiny new gadgets. Remember that God gives you strength for today and bright hopes for tomorrow, so "plug" yourself into His Word. Hang out with Christian friends, attend a Bible study, and worship regularly. Make sure you spend one-on-one time in prayer with the one who will keep you going and going strong – our Lord and Savior Jesus Christ.

TIME:OUT

CHAPTER **27** PSALM VERSE **14**

"Wait on the Lord; be of good courage and He shall strengthen your heart. Wait, I say, on the Lord!" (NJKV)

BODY
Rest, exercise, and eat nutritious food; they recharge your body and mind, allowing peak efficiency. Get plenty of each to stay fully charged.

SPIRIT
Share with God those things that are draining your strength physically, emotionally, and spiritually. Ask Him for help to overcome them.

MIND
Meditate on Psalm 27. Write your own short psalm. Journal what and how you must depend on the Lord in your life.

_____

_____

_____

_____

_____

_____

_____

_____

_____

_____

_____

_____

_____

Three Powerful Words— "I Was Wrong"

One of the greatest challenges for us athletes doesn't occur when we're sprinting down the field, court, or track. It occurs in our everyday walks as part of society. Too often, our egos cause us to become arrogant and treat others poorly. After my high school and college sports career ended, I attended a class reunion. There I saw several friends as well as a few classmates I had treated badly. Since I had seen them last, I had become serious about my Christian faith, but I'm sure they didn't know it (Why should they?). After some small talk, I simply said, "I'm sorry for being such a jerk." I didn't make any excuses and, surprisingly, each was forgiving, although I'm not sure I deserved their forgiveness.

In the Old Testament, God's people had become "jerks." Their arrogance and egos had caused God to remove His blessings and protection upon them, so they confessed and repented of their sins – Big Time! The book of Nehemiah records one of the most powerful acts of repentance in the Bible. Nehemiah says that God's people prayed and read continuously from the Holy Scripture for half a day! Are there some sins of arrogance that you need to take to God today? Do you need to go to God and those you have offended to say you're sorry?

TIME:OUT

CHAPTER 9

NEHEMIAH

VERSE 3

"They stood where they were and read from the Book of the Law of the Lord their God for a quarter of the day, and spent another quarter in confession and worshiping the Lord their God." (NIV)

CROSS TRAINING

BODY
Alternate running and/or biking between half-speed and full speed for cardio and leg strength. Half-speed keeps your heart rate up. A burst of full speed gives greater endurance and sprint speed.

SPIRIT
Pray that God would allow you to use sports as a way to glorify Him. Pray that the Holy Spirit would give you a spirit of humbleness and would remove the temptation for a puffed up ego and arrogant attitude.

MIND
Read Nehemiah 9:1–37. Relate this powerful prayer of forgiveness and praise to your own life, confess your sins, and list the many things God has done for you.

_____

_____

_____

_____

_____

_____

_____

_____

_____

_____

_____

_____

Be A Young Example

My freshman year of college football, I did everything I could think of to impress the coaching staff, hoping they would let me play. I was on the scout team, or the 'scrub squad' of players who saw little to no actual game time. Our job was to run plays with the starting team and prepare them for upcoming games. Once, during field goal practice, I leapt over a senior player, broke through the line, and blocked two kicks. All of this made the 1st string field goal team very angry, especially when the coaches started screaming at them. They were ready for the next play. When I attempted to break through the line again, the senior linemen hit me so hard I almost lost consciousness. The trainers had to give me smelling salts and hose me down with cool water to bring me around. However, my desire paid off, and I received a spot on the travel squad. I played in the next game.

The Apostle Paul encouraged a young disciple named Timothy in his walk of faith. He told Timothy to "let no one look down on you [him] because of your [his] youth." Even though he was young, he could set an example for all believers with his words and actions. It's important to remember that regardless of your age, both nonbelievers and followers of Christ can be influenced by your actions, attitude, love, and faith. Old or young, you can be an example with your desire to make a difference for Jesus Christ.

TIME:OUT

CHAPTER — **1 TIMOTHY** — VERSE

4 **12**

"Let no one despise your youth, but be an example to the believers in word, in conduct, in love, in spirit, in faith, in purity." (NKJV)

CROSS TRAINING

BODY
Give everything you've got, every minute you're practicing, whether you're on first string or on the bench. Remember someone is always watching your actions, and attitudes. Your efforts (or lack thereof) will determine how others perceive you and will directly relate to your athletic success.

SPIRIT
"...Train yourself to be Godly" (1 Tim 4:7). This week focus on daily praying, quiet time, or even fasting for 24 hours from all junk food *including* visual junk food on TV.

MIND
Read the "instructions to Timothy" in chapter 4 of 1 Timothy. List a few of Paul's instruction in your journal and make a notation of how you can (and will) follow them.

_____

_____

_____

_____

_____

_____

_____

_____

_____

_____

_____

_____

Bad Sports Blame Others

One of the most disturbing aspects of sports is the negative and boorish behavior of fans. As an athlete, fan, and even parent watching my children play, I've heard threats, profanities, and tantrums from adults. I've watched grown men scream at their kid's coaches and referees, blaming them for a loss (if you've ever been on the receiving end of some of this foolish behavior, I want you to know that it has nothing to do with you, but with much greater issues that these angry people must learn to cope with).

One of the most alarming events I have ever seen was the 2003 National League championship between the Chicago Cubs and the Florida Marlins. During the game, a Cubs fan tried to grab a foul ball, and he interfered with outfielder Moises Alou's efforts to catch it. What followed was a complete meltdown by the Cubs. They lost the lead, the game, and eventually the World Series hopes of their fans. Threats, profanities, and grown-up tantrums were leveled at the young man, a loyal Cub's fan and youth baseball coach. His life was almost ruined because fans blamed him for their team's lost focus.

Jesus once told his often emotional disciple Peter to focus on following His instruction and not to worry about His plans for another disciple. Too often we get caught up worrying about things that aren't really important, instead of focusing on what is important— obedience and service to Jesus Christ.

TIME:OUT

CHAPTER — **21** — JOHN — VERSE — **21**

'When Peter saw him, he said to Jesus, "Lord, what about him?" Jesus said to him, "If it is my will that he remain until I come, what is that to you? Follow me!"' (NRSV)

CROSS TRAINING

BODY

Work on concentration drills. Have someone yell and wave their hands in front of your while you practice your shots, catches, and other skills. It'll help with game-time focus.

SPIRIT

Pray for God's forgiveness for the times you've "dropped the ball." Forgive someone who has hurt you and/or broken your trust, and try to reinstate your friendship with him or her.

MIND

Read John 21. Note how Jesus forgave and reinstated Peter even after Peter had denied him (John 18:25-27). Journal how you can serve Christ this week - putting past mistakes behind you and focusing on God's plan for your life.

_____

_____

_____

_____

_____

_____

_____

_____

_____

_____

_____

_____

_____

Prepare for All Seasons

All good coaches and athletes know the importance of "off-season" training - that is working out and training to keep the body in top physical condition and skills sharp. One of the most well known practices (pun intended) of this premise is "Spring Ball." Spring Ball is when college football coaches get the opportunity to carefully evaluate the talent and skill level of each of their players without fall season's pressures of preparing for a game week after week. For the athlete, in addition to preparing for the upcoming season, it is a time that he or she can demonstrate his or her desire and ability to the coaching staff. It is a time for correction, encouragement, and rebuking to straighten out poor techniques and lack of discipline.

In Paul's letter to a younger disciple of Christ named Timothy, Paul coaches him on the importance of being prepared and the best way to coach other Christians who have not yet fully developed their understanding and practices of the faith. He stresses the importance and proper technique for correction, encouragement, and rebuking. Paul tells his protégé that there's some bad coaching out there (finish reading 2 Tim 4:2-5), but that Timothy must tough it out and sacrifice for the good of the team, and, most importantly, for the accurate spread and proclamation of God's uncompromising truth (as laid out for us in the Holy Bible).

TIME:OUT

CHAPTER 4

2 TIMOTHY

VERSE 2

"Preach the Word; be prepared in season and out of season; correct, rebuke and encourage with great patience and careful instruction." (NIV)

CROSS TRAINING

BODY
Maintain a regular workout schedule (minimum 4-5 times per week) even if you're not competing. Get with a coach, P. E. teacher, trainer etc. to design an effective exercise program.

SPIRIT
Get with a Christian friend and make a commitment to hold each other accountable for your walk with Jesus Christ. Agree to correct, encourage, and even rebuke each other, with patience and understanding.

MIND
Read 2 Timothy 4: 1-8. Note the athletic metaphors Paul uses when writing to Timothy about his faith. Journal some similarities between being a disciplined athlete and a committed Christian.

_____

_____

_____

_____

_____

_____

_____

_____

_____

_____

_____

_____

Step Outside of Your Comfort Zone

During his college career, my friend and co-author, Win Davis, gained notoriety as the oldest athlete in the NCAA to receive a full scholarship. He was also named his team's MVP. He worked as hard in the classroom as he did on the court and graduated # 1 in his class on his way to receiving a Master of Divinity degree. Win, who is white, also chose to study theology at a historically black university to have a faith experience different than he was used to. Since then, God has opened several doors for Win to serve and minister to people of very different backgrounds, ages, and interests. Win loves sport's ministry and young people, but wants to be able to share the Gospel of Jesus Christ with all people.

The Apostle Paul noted that although he was free from the influence of man due to his faith in Jesus Christ, he still became "all things to all people" so that he would be in a position to effectively share the Gospel. Don't be so focused on sports that you neglect your studies, community services, and relationships. Respect others who don't share your exact interests. Be prepared to go beyond your comfort zone to be "all things to all people" so that others can see the positive influence Jesus Christ has on your life.

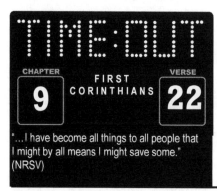

TIME:OUT

CHAPTER
9

FIRST
CORINTHIANS

VERSE
22

"...I have become all things to all people that I might by all means I might save some."
(NRSV)

CROSS TRAINING

BODY
Trying different physical activities may help you discover something you have a passion for, and may even prevent injuries. So no complaining in P.E. class when you have to try something new or grumbling when your group leader wants to do "goofy games" as an ice-breaker. Just think of it as cross-training.

SPIRIT
Pray for God to open doors for you to minister to (and with) those who are unlike you.

MIND
Read 1 Corinthians 9:19-27. Take a day this week and commit to not having your way. List some people who are not like you (i.e. elderly, those in need, different race, "unpopular" kids at school, etc.). Journal (and commit to) how you can serve them selflessly in the name of Christ, even if it's not 'your thing.'

_____

_____

_____

_____

_____

_____

_____

_____

_____

_____

_____

_____

Choose the Word Over the World

I've seen several athletes sacrifice everything in the hope of reaching the professional level. That's why the choice my friend and co-author, Calvin Duncan, made regarding his future in sports is almost unbelievable. After being named Conference Player of the year and All-American his senior year in college, Calvin was drafted by the NBA's Cleveland Cavaliers. Presented with the choice to play for the money and fame that accompanies professional sports or to answer God's call to pursue ministry, Calvin chose ministry despite the worldly advice of many who wanted him to play pro ball. As Calvin states, "I knew my success was only by the grace of God and choosing the game would have been solely about me. Had I pursued personal glory, I may have had a successful athletic career, but I would have fallen on my face doing what matters most – serving Jesus Christ."

When Jesus told his disciples that He must suffer and be killed, one of his closest friends, Peter, took Jesus aside and told Him not to do it. The Bible says Jesus then scolded Peter. He told Peter that he was focusing on the world when he should be focusing on God. Later, He warned his disciples not to grab for worldly things and, in the process, risk losing their eternal souls. What is more important - the world or the will of God?

TIME:OUT

CHAPTER
8

MARK

VERSE
36

"And how does a man benefit if he gains the whole world and loses his soul in the process?" (TLB)

BODY

Don't be persuaded by the will of advertisers that align themselves with sporting events and athletes. Don't indulge in the alcohol, sugary drinks, and junk food that companies are pushing just because they're 'official' sponsors. Did you know that the biggest sponsor of sporting events used to be cigarette companies until their deceptive advertising was exposed? That should give you a clue regarding the credibility between worldly companies and athletics.

SPIRIT

Each of us are given choices in our life whether to follow the will of God or the will of man. Pray for the guidance and the strength to choose God's will, even if you have to stand boldly before your family and friends.

MIND

Read Mark 8:31-38. Journal the things of the world that are getting in your way when it comes to following God's will, then write in front of each of them – "get behind me - - - - -."

_____

_____

_____

_____

_____

_____

_____

_____

_____

_____

_____

_____

_____

Weighted Down

Coach Linger was one of the best high school basketball coaches in West Virginia. He not only taught his teams how to play the game, but also the importance of self-discipline. Once, when his team was disrespecting a far less talented team, Coach Linger made his players wear the weighted vests they practiced in. While heavy vests improve strength and speed during practice, they are exhausting and make play far more challenging. Despite this handicap, Coach Linger's team actually won the game, but suffered under the weight of the vests. Coach told me he never had to lecture his players about treating others with respect again.

Jesus told His followers who were exhausted and weighed down by the concerns of the world to come to Him. He compared their problems to a yoke - a heavy wooden collar that farm animals wore to pull plows and carts, often full of heavy equipment. No doubt most people would associate a yoke with difficulty and exhaustion, but Jesus said His yoke was easy and burden light. He was saying that following Him is not a harsh set of rules (a message we need to take to our unbelieving friends), but that He is a gentle and understanding Savior. It's important that we know and share this truth about God's love. We may still experience hardships and heartbreaks in this world, but Jesus will never give His followers more than we can handle. Isn't it time you ask Jesus to truly be a major part of your life and let Him carry many of your concerns.

TIME·OUT

CHAPTER — **MATTHEW** — **VERSE**

11 **28**

"Take my yoke upon you, and learn from me: for I am gentle and humble in heart, and you will find rest for your souls." (NRSV)

BODY
If you work out regularly, adding weights to your body can enhance your strength training. To truly understand the expression "no pain, no gain," wear a weighted vest, belt, or ankle weights during low-impact exercises like pull-ups, dips, leg lifts etc.

SPIRIT
Pray right now, asking Jesus to lift those things that are weighing you down with worry.

MIND
Read Matthew 11: 20-30. We all struggle with our faith sometimes. Journal about those things that challenge you most, and then write out your prayers to God. Begin with, "God, I'm giving this to you!"

_____

_____

_____

_____

_____

_____

_____

_____

_____

_____

_____

_____

_____

_____

God Is At Every Game

When I was a student athlete at VA Union University, our men's basketball team was nationally ranked every year, and even played for the NCAA Division II National Championship. The gym was always packed to capacity for every game, and the games often made the front page of our local newspaper. I was a tennis player, however, and conversely, every tennis match was attended by only a handful of fans, friends, and family. Win or lose, our matches received only a few drops of ink in the tiny box score on the back page of the sports' section. Both teams played their hearts out, but my tennis team-mates and I received little attention.

Jesus emphasized the importance of every individual to God. He said that God knows every detail about us, even to the number of hairs on our heads (which I think is especially cool, since most people can barely see the hairs on my bald, shaved head). It's important for each of us to remember that whether we are playing in front of a full crowd or just a few folks, whether we're sitting in the stands, sitting on the bench, or sitting alone in our room, the Creator and Ruler of the Universe loved us so much that He sent His only Son to die for our sins and He and the very angels in Heaven cheer when we accept Jesus Christ as Lord and Savior. Like any good parent, our Heavenly Father is our biggest fan, and pays attention to our every word, our every thought, our every deed, and our every need.

TIME:OUT

CHAPTER — MATTHEW — VERSE

10 **30**

"He pays even greater attention to you, down to the last detail – even numbering the hairs on your head." (MSG)

CROSS TRAINING

BODY
If you really want to take your game and physical fitness to the next level, you need to work as hard when no one is watching as you do for attention from coaches, teammates, and fans. Commitment is the key.

SPIRIT
Ask God to help you notice all the needs around you. Pay attention, so that you can see the people who need encouraging words, helping hands, or good news of Jesus Christ's love.

MIND
Read Matthew 10:27-33. Journal about how God watches over you and guides you - even in tough times. Then, write some ways you can (and will) let another person know they too are important to God.

_____

_____

_____

_____

_____

_____

_____

_____

_____

_____

_____

_____

_____

Ugly Feet

"You have ugly feet," my daughter once observed when she saw my calloused, bruised feet and misaligned toes. Various sports injuries have taken their toll over time, including years of martial arts training under Sensei Arthur Drago. Well into his sixties, Sensei Drago has more athletic prowess than most men half his age. For almost half a century, he has been working out barefoot on hard wooden floors and kicking thousands of boards and cinder blocks. As a testament to all his hard work and training, he also has ugly feet.

Paul, referencing the prophet Isaiah, wrote about the beauty of "the feet of those who bring good news." I love The Living Bible's translation of Paul's letter to the church in Rome. He writes, "For the Scriptures tell us that no one who believes in Christ will ever be disappointed. Jews and Gentiles are the same in thus respect: they all have the same Lord who generously gives his riches to all those who ask him for them. Anyone who calls upon the name of the Lord will be saved. But how shall they ask him to save them unless they believe in him? And how can they believe in him if they have never heard about him? And how can they hear about him unless someone tells them? And how will anyone go and tell them unless someone sends him? That is what the Scriptures are talking about when they say, '*How beautiful are the feet of those who preach the Gospel of peace with God and bring glad tidings of good things.*' In other words, how welcome are those who come preaching God's Good News!"

My feet will never model footwear, but, if I carry the Good News of Jesus Christ to others, God will consider my feet beautiful. Let's follow in the footsteps of Jesus Christ today.

TIME:OUT

CHAPTER **10** ROMANS VERSE **15**

"And how can they preach unless they are sent? As it is written, "How beautiful are the feet of those who bring good news." (NIV)

BODY
From stretching to super-cardio shadow boxing to kicking, martial art moves have become very popular in fitness training. Play some high intensity music, warm up, and then throw a few hundred strikes and kicks at a punching bag (or imaginary opponent).

SPIRIT
Pray for the courage and opportunity to live and proclaim your faith, or "walk your talk." Ask God to reveal how your feet can carry the Good News of Jesus Christ to those who need to hear it.

MIND
Read Romans 10. It is one of the most powerful chapters in the Bible, combining the teaching of the Old Testament with the saving power of Jesus Christ. Now, read Isaiah 52. Journal your thoughts about how you can bring this good news of Jesus Christ to all who need to hear it

_____
_____
_____
_____
_____
_____
_____
_____
_____
_____
_____
_____

The Game Plan of Salvation

In both college and professional sports, there's a clock that ticks off the seconds in which a team is allowed to execute a play. In football, it's called a play clock. In basketball, it's a shot clock. In the NBA, for example, a team has 24 seconds to shoot and, hopefully, score. The ordinary fan often doesn't realize that every single second is important for setting up for the shot, and every single possession is important for setting up the team for victory. I have played and coached many games where victory or defeat depended on that very last possession. And many times, I could point to a specific play or possession that changed the momentum and ultimate outcome of the game.

Just like the 24 seconds to execute a play, there are 24 hours to execute a day – and believe it or not, every hour is important. You can waste time like the player who showboats with too much dribbling or fancy moves. You can be selfish like the player who forgets there's no 'I' in TEAM and plays to glorify himself. You can run out of gas like the player who hasn't put in the time to condition his or her body. You can mismanage your time like the player who doesn't use the clock effectively and, though scores, leaves plenty of time for the opponent to come back, score, and win the game. Or . . . you can live each day like the player who manages the clock effectively, gets his or her teammates involved, and realizes everyone's talent and knowledge is enhanced from great coaching.

The 24 hours in each day make up *"Life's Game Clock'* and how you manage your time decides whether you win or lose the game of life. But, more importantly, your time management will prepare you for 'Overtime' – where you will spend eternity.

Of all the sports analogies we have used throughout this book of devotions, **The Game Plan of Salvation** is by far the most important. It contains the steps necessary to have a personal relationship with Jesus Christ, and it includes a simple way to explain the Gospel (the *Good News*) of Jesus Christ to your friends, family, and teammates. You and all who have accepted Jesus Christ as Lord and Savior will spend eternity in Heaven on the greatest team ever assembled – the fellowship of believers.

First Quarter (God wants you on His team) – The greatest coach ever, God, wants you to be a champion. The Bible says that God told His followers, *"For I know the plans I have for you," declares the LORD, "plans to prosper you and not to harm you, plans to give you hope and a future"* (Jeremiah 29:11 NIV). He wants you so badly that he was willing to sacrifice His only son to open up a spot for you on His championship team. Jesus said, *"For God so loved the world that He gave His only begotten Son, that whoever believes in Him should not perish but have everlasting life"* (John 3:16 NKJV).

Second Quarter (Listen to Coach and No One Else) – The world will tell you there are other teams and paths to ultimate victory (i.e. eternity in Heaven), but Jesus said, *"I am the way and the truth and the life. No one comes to the Father except through me"* (John 14:6 NIV).

Third Quarter ("My Bad!") – Before you can learn and gain from your mistakes, you must realize that although you can improve, you will never be perfect. God's word says, *"There is none righteous, no, not one"* (Romans 3:10 NKJV) and *"all have sinned and fall short of God's glorious standard"* (Romans 3:23).

Fourth Quarter (Coming From Behind) – Our mistakes are costly, but God is there to give us a second chance. God's word says, *"For the wages of sin is death, but the gift of God is eternal life in Jesus Christ our Lord"* (Romans 6:23 NKJV). God put together a perfect game plan. Again the Bible says, *But God demonstrates His own love toward us, in that while we were still sinners, Christ died for us* (Romans 5:8 NKJV).

Overtime (The Game is on the Line and It's Up to You) – Wow! That seems like a lot of pressure, doesn't it? But you have the greatest coach ever, and all you have to do is ask for the winning play. Again the Bible says, *"because if you confess with your lips that Jesus is Lord and believe in your heart that God raised him from the dead, you will be saved* (Romans 10:9 NRSV)."

Celebrating the Victory...Forever!

"Can it really be that simple?" You may be thinking, or "With all the mistakes I've made, I don't deserve to be on God's team." And you are right. No one deserves God, but along with being the greatest coach that ever existed, God is also the most generous. The rewards in Heaven are greater than the most lucrative sport's contract or endorsement deal, and they will bring you more happiness. For, again, the Bible says, *"For by grace you have been saved through faith, and this is not your own doing; it is the gift of God-- not the result of works, so that no one may boast"* (Ephesians 2:8-9 NRSV).

Back to the Beginning – 24 Seconds Can Make the Difference.

Remember how we said how every second counts and how one 24 second play can be the difference between winning and losing? Well, if you're ready to make that decision to make God your life coach (Make Jesus Christ your Lord and Savior) all you have to do is pray a sincere and simple prayer. It takes about 24 seconds, but if you truly want to follow God, He will listen and save you from being separated from Him forever. Repeat these words:

"Dear Jesus. I am asking You to come into my heart and be my Lord and Savior. Please forgive me of my sins. Please send Your Holy Spirit to help me live the Christian life and follow the Bible that is God's Holy Word. I believe you died for me and God raised You from the dead. Thank you Jesus for saving my soul forever. Amen"

If you sincerely prayed to accept Jesus Christ as your Lord and Savior, you are what Jesus calls 'Born Again' (John 3:3). You are a new person in Christ. Now that doesn't mean you're now perfect. You will make mistakes because your soul still dwells in an imperfect body. But, it's important to stay strong in your Christian faith by praying and reading God's Word, alone and with other Christians in Bible study. It's also important that you find another strong Christian to hold you accountable for your actions.

Finally, you need to become part of the fellowship of believers called a church and find a place where Christians regularly come together to worship and praise God.

We are praying for you and excited about what God has planned for you!

Playing & praying in the name of Christ Jesus,
Calvin & Win

Win Davis
win@crosstraining4life.com

Calvin Duncan
rimnet5@gmail.com

About The Authors

Calvin Duncan is the senior pastor of The Faith and Family Church of Virginia. Raised on the tough streets of New Jersey, Calvin directed his energy into sports. He earned All-American honors as both a high school and college basketball player, and he led Virginia Commonwealth University to a conference championship and a Top 25 national ranking. The NBA's Cleveland Cavaliers later drafted him. Calvin has also coached in both the Continental Basketball Association and on the college level. His #5 jersey was retired by VCU, where he has also served as Life Coach.

Calvin also played with Athletes In Action, an international sport's ministry that travels throughout the world sharing the Gospel of Jesus Christ. He has mentored young people throughout the world through chapel services, Bible studies, and missions. Calvin has established youth centers, basketball camps and reading programs for underprivileged youth. He has been featured in numerous magazines and newspaper articles, as well as other media like video and television, as an outstanding athlete, community activist and Christian. He and his wife, Barbara, have three children.

Win Davis is the pastor to youth and young adults at Cambridge Baptist Church in Virginia. He is also the founder of CrossTraining4Life, a ministry that challenges Christian athletes to take their faith to the fields of play and to develop their bodies, minds, and spirits for personal growth and Christian service.

Win entered college on a football scholarship, eventually earned a starting position but suffered a season-ending injury. He assumed his college athletic career was over, but God had other plans. More than twenty-five years after earning his first scholarship, Win became the oldest player in the NCAA to receive a full athletic scholarship when he answered God's call to enter the ministry and pursue a master of divinity degree at Virginia Union University. Given a second chance, Win was named co-captain and Most Valuable Player of his tennis team, was nominated for Academic All-American and graduated #1 in his class. Win also has a degree in communication from James Madison University. He has served as an adjunct professor, communication consultant and event speaker for Christian and secular organizations. He is author of *Reach for the Stars Without Losing Your Balance.* Win and his wife, Debbie, have two daughters.